MUHAMMAD
(Salla Allahu 'alaihi wa sallam)

The Last Prophet

CHILDREN'S SERIES

JUNIOR LEVEL - PART II

(Madinah Period)

Dr. 'Alia N. Athar

LIBRARY OF ISLAM, P. O. Box 1923, Des Plaines, IL   60017-19239 (U.S.A)

PUBLISHER:

LIBRARY OF ISLAM
P.O. Box 1923
Des Plaines, IL 60017 (U.S.A.)

DISTRIBUTOR:

KAZI PUBLICATIONS INC.
3023 West Belmont Avenue
Chicago, IL 60618 (U.S.A.)

COPYRIGHT © LIBRARY OF ISLAM 1987

All rights reserved. No part of this book may be reproduced or utilized in any form or by any means, electronic or mechanical, including photocopying and recording or by any information storage and retrieval system, without the written permission of the publisher. All inquiries may be sent to Library of Islam, Des Plaines, IL 60017.

Library Of Congress Cataloging In Publishing Data

MUHAMMAD, The Last Prophet 11

Athar, Alia N.

ARTWORK: MUBARAK ZAMAN

TYPESETTING:

A-1 TYPESETTERS, CHICAGO

ISBN : 0-934905-04-5

Manufactured in the United States of America.

CONTENTS

Author's Note..4
Foreword..5
Chapter 1   Light of True Faith................................9
Chapter 2   The City of the Messenger..................13
Chapter 3   Masjid-Un-Nabawi................................16
Chapter 4   Living Peacefully..................................21
Chapter 5   Difference in Saying and Doing............24
Chapter 6   We Are Strong and Powerful................28
Chapter 7   The Day of Glory..................................31
Chapter 8   Fighting Again......................................34
Chapter 9   Peace is Better Than War....................38
Chapter 10   Victory of the Muslims........................41
Chapter 11   Invitation to Islam................................46
Chapter 12   Return to Makkah................................48
Chapter 13   Mercy to the World..............................51
Chapter 14   Mission Completed..............................54
Chapter 15   The Farewell Speech............................58
              Sayings of Rasulullah..........................62

AUTHOR'S NOTE

Praise be to Compassionate and Merciful Allah, Who grants His Favor and Mercy to us. It is He, Who judges and it is to Him that we return.

The objective of this book is to acquaint the children with the knowledge of the life-history of Rasulullah (s.a.w.) in a systematic and stimulating way. The first and the second parts of the book cover the Makkah and Madinah periods respectively. It is a text-book on Sirah and is recommended for the children in the age-group of 6-9 years.

The book contains controlled vocabulary. Some essential Arabic terminology has been introduced. Parents and teachers are urged to pay special attention to the indoctrination of correct pronunciation of the Islamic terminology in this highly impressionable phase of the development of the children. The words of blessing for the Prophet (s.a.w.) have been used throughout the text. They have, however, been omitted from the titles so as not to cause undue burden for the young minds while reading the text. For the same reasons, words of blessing have been omitted from some other places. Parents and teachers are advised to use them orally.

Wa ma tawfiqi illa billah (and my success in my task can only come from Allah).

Dr. 'Alia N. Athar

FOREWORD

IN THE NAME OF ALLAH, THE BENEFICENT, THE MERCIFUL

It is heartening to note that in recent years, there has been a marked expansion of the Muslim community in the West. The universal nature of Islam and its emphasis on the practical aspects which encompasses the total life of the individual has been the driving force during this whole process. It would not be an overestimate to say that the Muslims in the West are taking a leading role in transforming the world into a peaceful abode for everybody. No doubt, the present crisis in the world is the result of distancing ourselves too much from the spiritual aspects of our existence.

To reach the lofty goal of existing in a peaceful world, it is important that the essence of the religion of Islam be internalized in its truest sense. This requires the wide urgency of availability of Islamic literature in this environment. Although attention has been directed towards this end and some work has been done, there is a visible dearth of appropriate literature for children and youth. They are growing up in an atmosphere which is distinctly different from the one in which their parents grew up. They have specific needs, which require specific attention.

It is now time for this issue to be addressed properly, before our young generation is totally alienated from their religious background. In a society, where an adolescent is exposed to a variety of experiences, an awareness of his/her religious and cultural heritage is but a deterrent to his/her being lost in the conflicting milieu. It is incumbent upon us to help the Muslim children and youth to understand and relate to themselves and others so as to exist as healthy and productive human beings, making optimal contribution to the well-being of the society.

With a demanding new generation of Muslims, reaching the stage of adolescence, the task of educating them becomes a major responsibility of the parents. Also, it puts an enormous strain on the intellectual sources of the community. The challenge lies with the Muslim educationists who must measure up to the task of introducing the basics of Islam to children growing up in a changing, challenging and complex world. They have to make the material so appealing that it draws immediate attention of the inquisitive child of this age and enhances and motivates learning.

This work is a part of the series of books that Dr. 'Alia N. Athar aspires to present to the young readers. I am confident that her knowledge and expertise in the field and her commitment and devotion to the task would enable her to carry on her plan successfully. Her endeavors to contribute to the training of young minds are highly appreciable. I believe that the books in this series would be of great value.

I pray to Almighty Allah to help the author in bringing this series to completion and make it beneficial for the community.

Rajab 27, 1407
March 28, 1987

Dr. 'Abdullah 'Omar Naseef
Secretary General
Rabitat al-Alam al-Islami
Makkah al-Mukarramah
Kingdom of Saudi Arabia

TO

CHILDREN EVERYWHERE

Surat ul-Fatiha

CHAPTER 1

LIGHT OF TRUE FAITH

The Muslims of Yathrib knew that Rasulullah (s.a.w.) was on his way to their city. With great excitement they awaited his arrival. Finally, the day came when he arrived in the company of Abu Bakr.

The whole of Yathrib was filled with joy. All of the Muslims were cheerful. The Muslims of Makkah had left their homes to follow the Messenger of Allah (s.a.w.). Now he was with them.

The Muslims of Madinah had eagerly waited for Rasulullah (s.a.w.). Most of them had not seen him before. Now, they could see him. It was the happiest day for all of them. They thanked Allah again and again.

All the men, women and children came out of their houses. It was like a festival in the city. The children were wearing beautiful clothes and they were singing songs:

> The full moon rises on us,
> from the Hill of Wada'.
> You brought the light for all of us.
> You brought the light of true faith.
> We will always obey you.
> We will always thank Allah.

When the children came near Rasulullah (s.a.w.), he smiled and said: "I love all of you." He was always very kind to children.

Every Muslim in Yathrib wanted Rasulullah (s.a.w.) to be his guest. Everyone loved him. Rasulullah (s.a.w.) did not want to hurt anybody's feelings, so he said: "I'll stay at the place where my she-camel stops."

The she-camel stopped near the house of Abu Ayyub al-Ansari. He and his wife were very happy. "Allah has blessed us," they said. Rasulullah (s.a.w) stayed there.

Word Watch

cheerful	beautiful	eagerly	festival
Wada'	faith	guest	

Thinking It Over

A. Make a circle around T (true) or F (false).

1. The Muslims of Yathrib welcomed the Messenger of Allah (s.a.w.)   **T / F**

2. Rasulullah (s.a.w.) did not like to hurt anybody's feelings.   **T / F**

3. Rasulullah (s.a.w.) decided to stay with Abu Tamim.   **T / F**

4. Rasulullah (s.a.w.) liked children very much.   **T / F**

5. Rasulullah (s.a.w.) reached Yathrib with a group of many Muslims.   **T / F**

B. Fill in the blanks with the words given.

The children of Yathrib were singing a beautiful --------- when Rasulullah (s.a.w.) reached there. He was -------------- to see them. When they came to him, he told them that he -------------- all children.

(loved, song, happy)

بِسْمِ اللهِ الرَّحْمٰنِ الرَّحِيْمِ

CHAPTER 2

THE CITY OF THE MESSENGER

The new name of Yathrib was Madinat-ur-Rasul, the City of the Messenger. It is usually called Madinah.

Madinah was very different from Makkah. Rasulullah (s.a.w.) preached Islam in Makkah for thirteen years, but the people there were quite afraid of their leaders. They obeyed their leaders and treated Rasulullah (s.a.w.) and his followers badly.

The people of Madinah were hospitable and wise. They understood that Rasulullah (s.a.w.) was truthful. They were very happy to accept Islam and help Allah's Messenger (s.a.w.).

Rasulullah (s.a.w.) called the Muslims of Madinah, Ansar, the helpers. The Muslims from Makkah were called, Muhajirun, the people who left their homes for their religion.

Rasulullah gathered all of the Muslims and said:
"O, Muslims! you are all brothers in Islam, you must love one another. Allah is happy with those who care

for one another.

> The Ansar told the Makkan Muslims:
>> You are our brothers. You've left everything in Makkah for Islam. Madinah is your new home. Everything that belongs to us, belongs to you.

> The Ansar were great people. They were very good and very generous to their Muslim brothers.

> The Makkan Muslims said:
>> "May Allah bless you, our brothers, we will work hard to earn our bread, we will not be a burden on you."

> Rasulullah (s.a.w.) was happy with all of them. They were great Muslims. They obeyed Allah and His Messenger completely. They did everything to make Islam strong.

****

Word Watch

belong	Muhajirun	generous	burden
Ansar	hospitable		

Thinking It Over

A. Circle the correct answer.

1. The people of Yathrib changed the name of their city because--------------
    a. it had become a big city.
    b. they did not like its old name.
    c. Rasulullah (s.a.w.) told them to do so.
    d. Rasulullah (s.a.w.) had come to live there.

2. Ansar were the people who--------------
    a. belonged to the city of Yathrib.
    b. belonged to the city of Makkah.
    c. belonged to the city of Ta'if.

3. The Ansar told the Muslims of Makkah:--------------
    a. "you must bring your wealth from Makkah."
    b. "you'll share everything that we have."
    c. "we cannot give you anything."

4. The Muhajirun were the people who--------------
    a. came to live in Makkah.
    b. came to live in Madinah.
    c. lived in the south of Arabia.

CHAPTER 3

MASJID-UN-NABAWI

Rasulullah (s.a.w.) bought some land and built a Masjid in Madinah. All of the Muslims helped him. This Masjid is called Masjid-un-Nabawi. Muslims from all over the world love to go to Madinah to pray in that Masjid.

After they had completed the Masjid, they built some rooms beside it. Rasulullah (s.a.w.) lived there. The rooms were very small and were made of stone and mud bricks.

Rasulullah (s.a.w.) sat on the floor, on a simple mat of date leaves. He met with the Muslims there and taught them Islam.

He was the leader of the Muslims. But he was very humble. When the people from other places came to see him, they were surprised to see how simply he lived.

There were some poor Muslims, who had no families. Rasulullah (s.a.w.) gave them a place in the Masjid.

They stayed there and prayed most of the time. They were known as Ashab-us-Suffah.

It was wonderful. There were no Kuffar to stop the Muslims from performing Salat. They had their own Masjid, where they performed Salat, learned about Islam, and met with their brothers.

But they needed something more. They had to perform Salat five times a day. What if they forgot its time? There had to be some way to remind the Muslims about the time of Salat.

Rasulullah (s.a.w.) came up with an idea. He asked his Sahabi (Companion), Bilal, to call Adhan. Bilal had a beautiful voice.
The Muslims felt great to hear the Adhan:
    Allahu Akbar, Allahu Akbar (Allah is Great, Allah is Great), ---------------
La ilaha illa Allah (there is no diety but Allah).

****

Word Watch

Masjid-un-Nabawi	attached	surprise
Ashab-us-Suffah	perform	Adhan
La ilaha illa Allah	Bilal	bricks
Allahu Akbar	Companion	diety

Masjid-un-Nabawi (Outside View)

Thinking It Over

A. Make a circle around T (true) or F (false).

1. Rasulullah (s.a.w.) alone built the Masjid at Madinah. **T / F**

2. The people from other places were surprised to see how rich Rasulullah (s.a.w.) was. **T / F**

3. Rasulullah (s.a.w.) lived in a palace in Madinah. **T / F**

4. Ashab-us-Suffah were the people who lived in Masjid-un-Nabawi. **T / F**

5. The first Sahabi to call Adhan was Bilal. **T / F**

B. Fill in the blanks with the words given.

The Muslims were --------------- to have their own ---------------, where they could perform Salat. It was the place where they could --------------- about Islam.

(Masjid, learn, happy)

The Bilal Masjid (Makkah)

CHAPTER 4

LIVING PEACEFULLY

Rasulullah (s.a.w.) was the kindest man. He wanted all people to live in peace. He never liked wars. He never liked to see people fighting and suffering.

Although most of the people of Madinah became Muslims, there were some people believing in other religions. Some of them understood that Muhammad (s.a.w.) was the same prophet, about whom their holy books had told them. They became Muslims.

Some of them did not want to accept Islam.
Rasulullah (s.a.w.) told them:
> Let's make Madinah a city of peace. Let's not be enemies of each other. We can have different religions and still be good to each other. Let's live together peacefully and happily.

All of them agreed to this. They said:
> "We'll live together peacefully. We won't hurt each other. If an enemy attacks our city, we'll defend it together."

Everyone was happy. There was no more fighting, and no more suffering. The Muslims and the non-Muslims together said to Rasulullah (s.a.w.): "You've brought peace and happiness to us. You've made our city beautiful."

****

Word Watch

defend   happily   enemy   attack

Thinking It Over

A. Circle the correct answer.

1. The city of Madinah had---------------
   a. only Muslim people.
   b. people from different religions.
   c. only idol-worshippers.

2. Rasulullah (s.a.w.) told the people who did not want to become Muslims:---------------
   a. "You must leave Madinah."
   b. "You must accept Islam, otherwise we cannot live together peacefully."
   c. "You can follow your religion and we can live together peacefully."

3. The non-Muslims of Madinah told the Muslims: "If an enemy attacks Madinah,---------------
   a. we'll help you in defending it."
   b. we'll leave the city."
   c. we'll help your enemies."

CHAPTER 5

DIFFERENCE IN SAYING AND DOING

"Allahu Akbar, Allahu Akbar," Madinah sounded with the praise of Allah five times every day.

Many people from other places came to Madinah. They accepted Islam and returned to their homes.

During all this period, Angel Jibreel was bringing the parts of al-Qur'an, the sacred book, to Rasulullah (s.a.w.). Whenever some Wahi came, Rasulullah (s.a.w.) told his Ashab about it. Some of the Ashab memorized it and others wrote it down.

They learned more and more about Islam, the way to live happily in this world, and in the Akhirah (Hereafter).

The Muslims love to read al-Qur'an. It gives them a lot of knowledge. They like to learn it by heart. One who learns all of it by heart is called Hafiz.

There were some people in Madinah who thought

they were superior to others. They did not want to believe in a prophet, who was from another tribe. They did not like Rasulullah (s.a.w.). They wanted to harm the Muslims.

There were some other people, who did not like the teachings of Islam. They still believed in idolatry. They also became the enemies of the Muslims. They thought of a trick and said:

> Let's go to the Muslims and lie to them. We'll tell them that we are Muslims, and we are your brothers. They'll trust us. Then, we can harm them easily.

Al-Qur'an warns the Muslims about such people. It calls them, Munafiqun, those who say one thing, and do something else.

When the Munafiqun met with the Muslims, they said: "We are with you." When they were with their own group, they made fun of the Muslims. They made plans to make the Muslims weak.

****

Word Watch

sounded	period	sacred	Akhirah
Hereafter	Hafiz	trick	Munafiqun
Wahi	Ashab		

Thinking It Over

A. Make a circle around T (true) or F (false).

1. The Munafiqun are the people who do not do what they say. **T / F**

2. Akhirah means the life in this world. **T / F**

3. One who learns all of al-Qu'ran is called Sahabi. **T / F**

4. Al-Qur'an gives us a lot of knowledge. **T / F**

3. Some of the people of Madinah thought they were superior to others. **T / F**

Ghamamah Masjid (Madinah)

CHAPTER 6

WE ARE STRONG AND POWERFUL

The Kuffar of Makkah said angrily: "How can Muhammad escape us? How can he keep on talking against our idols? How can he preach his religion freely?"

They heard that many more people of Madinah had accepted Islam. So their anger increased.

One Makkan said:
>We must not let Muhammad live peacefully and preach his religion. We must not let Muslims become strong. We are more powerful than them. We can crush them easily.

They made plans to attack the Muslims of Madinah. Their leaders got together and talked about this. Their poets wrote poems against the Muslims. Their rich people gave a lot of money to buy arms and horses for the battle.

All of this to punish the Muslims, to stop them from worshipping Allah and to make them worship idols again.

The Munafiqun in Madinah heard about it. They became happy. "We'll help the Makkans," they said to one another.

The Muslims heard that the Makkans wanted to attack them. Some of them got worried. They had no wealth to buy arms and horses. Many of them were new in Madinah. They were working hard to earn their living.

"The Kuffar are many and they are much richer than us," they thought.

Most of the Muslims had strong faith in Allah. They said:

> We are not afraid of the Kuffar. Almighty Allah is the Greatest. He's more powerful than the Kuffar. He's with us.

****

Word Watch

escape　　　increase　　　arms　　　horse

Thinking It Over

A. Circle the correct answer.

1. The Kuffar were very angry because the Muslims ----------------
    a. had taken all their wealth.
    b. were practicing Islam freely in Madinah.
    c. wanted to return to Makkah.

2. The Muslims of Madinah were not afraid of the Kuffar because ----------------
    a. they had a large army.
    b. they had enough money to buy arms.
    c. they had faith in Allah.

B. Fill in the blanks with the words given.

The Makkans wanted to ---------------- Madinah because they were ---------------- with the Muslims. They did not want to let the ---------------- follow Prophet Muhammad (s.a.w.).

(angry, attack, people)

CHAPTER 7

THE DAY OF GLORY

Rasulullah (s.a.w.) prayed:

O Allah, the proud Kuffar have come to defeat us and to show the world that Your Prophet is a liar. If this small force of Islam is crushed, there would be no one to worship you. Give us victory, O our Creator!

The Kuffar were coming towards Madinah, with an army of one thousand soldiers. They had a lot of arms and many horses. The Muslims said:

All of us are with you, O, Rasulullah! We are not afraid of the Kuffar. Allah will help us. He's the most powerful. We'll defend our city bravely.

They came out of Madinah to fight the enemy. Rasulullah (s.a.w.) was their commander. There were only three hundred and thirteen people, with very few arms and two horses.

They fought with the Kuffar at Badr, some miles away from Madinah. Abu Jahal, the commander of the Kuffar was killed. Many other Kuffar were also killed and many injured.

The Kuffar were shocked. They ran back to Makkah. They could not understand what had happened. The Muslims army had very few soldiers. How could it be so powerful?

The Muslims won the battle, only with Allah's help. Al-Qur'an calls this day, Yawm-ul-Furqan, the Day of Glory.

The Battle of Badr showed that if Muslims obey Allah and have trust in Him, they will win.

Islam is a religion of peace. It does not preach war. But it asks Muslims to fight bravely if they are attacked.

****

Word Watch

victory	soldier	Badr	bravely
shocked	glory	Yawm-ul-Furqan	

Thinking It Over

A. Make a circle around T (true) or F (false).

1. The Battle of Badr was the first battle between the Muslims and the Kuffar. **T / F**

2. The Makkans had an army of five hundred people in the Battle of Badr. **T / F**

3. Rasulullah (s.a.w.) was the commander of the Muslim army. **T / F**

4. Badr is in the city of Madinah. **T / F**

5. The Muslims won the Battle of Badr with Allah's help. **T / F**

CHAPTER 8

FIGHTING AGAIN

The whole of Makkah was sad. The Kuffar were ashamed. They had thought that they would kill all Muslims. They had thought that there would be no Islam in the world. But it did not happen. The Muslims won the battle.

They went to Ka'bah and complained to their idols. "O our gods, we lost to the Muslims, why didn't you help us?"

How could the idols help them? They could not even help themselves.

Abu Sufyan, the Makkan leader told them:
> O my people! Don't be sad, don't be ashamed. We'll not spare the Muslims. We'll attack them again. We'll punish them strongly.

All other leaders agreed with Abu Sufyan. For one year, they prepared themselves. They took help from other tribes. Then, they returned to fight again.

There were three thousand strong soldiers. All of them had swords and other arms.

Rasulullah (s.a.w.) heard about this big army. He gathered the Muslims. They were few, they were poor, but their faith was very strong. No one was afraid. They were ready to fight bravely, to save the city of Islam.

One thousand Muslims were ready to fight with the enemy. The Makkans reached Uhud, which is a mountain outside Madinah.

Both armies stood face to face. Abdullah ibn Ubayy, the leader of the Munafiqun, was in the Muslim army. He had three hundred men in his command.

"This is a good time to cheat the Muslims," he thought, "I'll take my men out and the Makkans will win the battle easily." He left the field with three hundred soldiers. The Muslims knew that he was the leader of the Munafiqun.

In spite of that, the Kuffar could not win the Battle of Uhud. They could not enter Madinah. Allah saved it. The enemy returned to Makkah.

Word Watch

ashamed	happen	Abu Sufyan
prepare	Uhud	field

Thinking It Over

A. Circle the correct answer.

1. The Kuffar were ashamed because ---------------
    a. they could not defeat the Muslims.
    b. their army was too small.
    c. they were poor people.

2. Abu Sufyan told the Makkans ---------------
    a. "We'll never attack the Muslims again."
    b. "We'll attack the Muslims again."
    c. "It was our mistake to attack the Muslims."

3. In the Battle of Uhud, the number of the Muslims was ---------------
    a. three hundred.
    b. one thousand.
    c. eight thousand.

Mount Uhud (Outside Madinah)

CHAPTER 9

PEACE IS BETTER THAN WAR

"We've fought two battles with the Muslims. But we couldn't harm them. We must fight again to destroy them," the Kuffar said.

They asked all of the people of Arabia to help them. They became stronger. Two years after the Battle of Uhud, they left Makkah to attack Madinah for the third time.

This time, they had a huge army. Many other tribes of Arabia had joined them. The non-Muslims living in Madinah had a peace treaty with the Muslims. But they helped the enemy of the Muslims. They broke their treaty.

"Let's dig trenches to save the city," Salman al-Farsi said. Rasulullah (s.a.w.) liked this advice. It was a new method to defend the city. It took them one month to dig the trenches.

When the Kuffar reached Madinah, they were surprised to see the trenches. They could not enter Madinah. For many days, they attacked the city, but the Muslims did not let them enter the city. They fought bravely.

While the Kuffar were trying hard, a thunderstorm came. All their tents were blown away. Everything was gone, even their food. They ran back to their homes. The Muslims won the battle. Surely, Allah had helped them. This is known as the Battle of Khandaq (trench).

Now, the Makkans knew that they could not destroy Islam. Some of them became sure that Allah was helping the Muslims. They accepted Islam and prayed to Allah to forgive them.

A year after this battle, Rasulullah (s.a.w.) decided to visit Ka'bah. Many of the Ashab got ready to go with him. They began their journey and reached near Makkah.

The Makkans did not let them enter the city. They said: "Let's make a peace treaty now, you can come next year and visit Ka'bah." Rasulullah (s.a.w.) said: "Peace is better than war. Let's make the peace treaty."

Word Watch

destroy	treaty	trench
Khandaq	tent	Salman al-Farsi

Thinking It Over

A. Make a circle around T (true) or F (false).

1. In the Battle of Khandaq, many tribes of Arabia helped the Makkans. **T / F**

2. Salman al-Farsi advised the Muslims to dig trenches. **T / F**

3. Digging trenches was an old method of defending a city in Arabia. **T / F**

4. The Kuffar stayed in the Battle-field in spite of the storm. **T / F**

5. Rasulullah (s.a.w.) made a peace treaty with the Makkans. **T / F**

CHAPTER 10

VICTORY OF THE MUSLIMS

Almighty Allah had ordered His Messenger (s.a.w.) to preach Islam everywhere. Now, it was easy for the Messenger to obey Allah's order. The Makkans had stopped their attacks on Madinah.

Many people came to Madinah to learn about Islam. Many people became Muslims. They gave up their bad deeds. They followed Rasulullah (s.a.w.).

Khaybar is a town in the north of Madinah. The tribes living there had promised the Muslims to help them if they were attacked.

But they broke their promise. In the Battle of Khandaq, they helped the Kuffar of Makkah in their attack on Madinah.

When they saw that the Kuffar could not crush the Muslims, they made their own plan to attack Madinah and destroy the Muslims.

Rasulullah (s.a.w.) came to know about their plan.

Once again, Madinah was in danger and the Muslims had to fight again.

The Muslims marched towards Khaybar where the enemy had very strong forts. They saw that their army was too small to attack the forts. But they had trust in Almighty Allah. All of them fought bravely. The battle took many days.

Ali ibn Abu Talib was famous for his bravery. He entered the strongest fort of the enemy. After that, all other forts fell.

The Muslims won the battle with the help of Allah. The Khaybar tribes could not destroy the Muslims. This battle is known as the Battle of Khaybar.

* * * * * * * * * * * * * * * * * * *

Word Watch

Khaybar   fort   Ali ibn Abu Talib

Forts of Khaybar

Thinking It Over

A. Circle the correct answer.

1. Rasulullah's duty was to spread Islam ---------------
   a. only in Arabia.
   b. only in Makkah.
   c. everywhere.

2. The Muslims fought with the tribes of Khaybar because ---------------
   a. they wanted to destroy the Muslims.
   b. they were very rich people.
   c. they were very weak people.

3. The Sahabi who broke the door of the strongest fort was ---------------
   a. Salman al-Farsi.
   b. Bilal ibn Ribah.
   c. Ali ibn Abu Talib.

4. In the Battle of Khaybar, ---------------
   a. the Muslims were defeated.
   b. no army was successful.
   c. the Muslims defeated the enemy.

A Letter of the Prophet (s.a.w.)

CHAPTER 11

INVITATION TO ISLAM

Muhammad Rasulullah (s.a.w.) was sent as the Messenger for all humankind. Islam is the religion for the whole world.

Rasulullah (s.a.w.) sent letters to the kings of the neighboring countries. He wrote:

> The people who follow the true religion are the blessed ones. I invite you to Islam. You shall be safe if you accept it.
>
> Believe in Allah as the Only God. Do not take others as gods. I am the Messenger of Allah. Please listen to what I say. It is the Message of Allah. Peace be upon him, who follows the true guidance.

Some of the kings were happy with his letter. Others were unhappy. They were proud kings. They thought they were the most powerful, they did not want to think about the Creator. Allah does not like the people who are proud.

Word Watch

humankind   king   countries   letter

Thinking It Over

A. Make a circle around T (true) or F (false).

1. Rasulullah (s.a.w.) ordered the neighboring kings to come to him. **T / F**

2. All of the kings were happy to receive Rasulullah's letter. **T / F**

3. The people who follow the true religion have the blessings of Allah. **T / F**

4. Allah likes the people who are not proud. **T / F**

5. No one is more powerful than Allah. **T / F**

CHAPTER 12

RETURN TO MAKKAH

Ater the peace treaty with the Makkans, many more people became Muslims. Islam was spreading everywhere. Rasulullah (s.a.w.) sent more Ashab to different places to tell the people about Islam and to teach them al-Qur'an.

The Makkans did not like this. They were still the enemies of the Muslims. They were still thinking of ways to harm them. They said: "Let's break the treaty. Then we can fight with the Muslims again."

They found a way to break the treaty. They helped a tribe in killing some people. They were not supposed to do that. The people they had killed were the friends of the Muslims.

Rasulullah (s.a.w.) was unhappy with this. He sent a letter to the leaders of the Kuffar. They answered that they wanted to break the peace treaty and they were ready to fight with the Muslims.

The Muslims were angry about the killing of their friends. The time had come for the Muslim army to march to Makkah. A large number of Muslims got ready for the march. When they reached Makkah, the Makkans were scared.

The Muslims had their camps outside the city. In the darkness of the night, Abu Sufyan came to see Rasulullah (s.a.w.).

He was the leader of the Kuffar. He was quite afraid. Rasulullah (s.a.w.) forgave him for what he had done to the Muslims.

Abu Sufyan heard the words of Rasulullah (s.a.w.). He could not believe his ears. He was surprised for a while. He could not imagine that Rasulullah (s.a.w.) would be so kind and forgiving. He accepted Islam and became a Muslim.

****

Word Watch

camp   darkness   suppose

Thinking It Over

A. Circle the correct answer.

1. The Kuffar broke the peace treaty because ---------------
    a. they wanted to fight with the Muslims.
    b. the Muslims had killed their friends.
    c. the Muslims had threatened them.

2. When the Makkans saw the Muslim army, they were ---------------
    a. angry.
    b. frightened.
    c. happy.

3. When Rasulullah (s.a.w.) saw Abu Sufyan, he ---------------
    a. punished him.
    b. told him to go away.
    c. forgave him.

4. Abu Sufyan was surprised when he saw ---------------
    a. how strong the Muslim army was.
    b. how weak the Muslim army was.
    c. how forgiving the Prophet (s.a.w.) was.

CHAPTER 13

MERCY TO THE WORLD

The Makkans could not sleep that night. They remembered the days when they used to torture the Muslims. They remembered the bad words that they had said to Rasulullah (s.a.w.). They remembered that they had forced the Muslims to leave their homes.

"How could we be so cruel? How could we be so foolish?" some of them thought. Now the Muslims had returned. and were very powerful. Their faith was stronger and they were not afraid of anyone except Allah. Surely, Allah was helping them.

The Makkans shut themselves inside their houses. They could not face the Muslims. They could not attack them any more.

"O Makkans!" Abu Sufyan announced, "Don't be afraid of Muhammad. He doesn't want to hurt anyone. You should trust him. The Muslims don't want to fight.

with you. They are peace loving people."

Rasulullah (s.a.w.) entered Makkah. Every Muslim was saying: "Allahu Akbar, Allahu Akbar." It was a wonderful scene to watch.

Rasulullah (s.a.w.) made a speech:

> O, people of Makkah! you should not be proud of your color or your tribe. We are all children of Adam. You should be good to one another. Today, I forgive all of you for what you did to us.

The Kuffar were quite surprised. Only a true prophet could be so good, so kind and so generous. All of them accepted Islam. Rasulullah (s.a.w.) is a mercy for all humankind.

Rasulullah (s.a.w.) went to Ka'bah and smashed all of the idols. Now, Ka'bah was clean for the worship of Allah. The Muslims thanked Allah for His help. Then, they performed Salat there.

****

Word Watch

remember   announce   scene   speech   Adam   Salat

Thinking It Over

A. Make a circle around T (true) or F (false).

1. The Makkans welcomed the Muslim army when it came to Makkah. **T / F**

2. The Makkans remembered that they had tortured the Muslims. **T / F**

3. All of the Makkans came out to fight with the Muslims. **T / F**

4. The Kuffar broke all of the idols which were in Ka'bah. **T / F**

5. All of the Makkans became Muslims. **T / F**

B. Fill in the blanks with the words given.

The Makkans were scared when the --------------- entered Makkah. They stayed inside their ---------------. Prophet Muhammad (s.a.w.) said: "I forgive all of you." The Makkans were quite ---------------.

(surprised, Muslims, houses)

CHAPTER 14

MISSION COMPLETED

Now, Makkah was a city of Islam. All of the People there were Muslims. They were a part of the Ummah. Rasulullah (s.a.w.) had forgiven all of them. All of them were happy to become Muslims.

Rasulullah (s.a.w.) and his Companions returned to Madinah. The whole of Arabia knew about the success of Islam in Makkah. People from all over Arabia came to visit Rasulullah (s.a.w.).

The people of Ta'if had treated Rasulullah (s.a.w.) rudely. They had turned him out of their city. Now, they sent some people to Madinah, to learn about the true religion. Then, all of them became Muslims. Rasulullah (s.a.w.) had prayed for this. Allah had listened to the prayer of His beloved Prophet (s.a.w.).

Rasulullah (s.a.w.) sent more of his Companions to the different parts of Arabia and its neighboring countries. Their job was to teach al-Qur'an to the people and explain to them the teachings of Islam.

Rasulullah (s.a.w.) taught Islam for twenty three years, thirteen years in Makkah and ten years in Madinah.

Almost all of Arabia had become Muslim. Every day, more and more people accepted Islam as their way of life. The Last Messenger of Allah (s.a.w.) had completed his mission. He had told humankind about Islam, the way to truth and peace.

****

Word Watch

beloved explain scene Ummah

Thinking It Over

A. Make a circle around T (true) or F (false).

1. The Prophet (s.a.w.) stayed at Makkah after it became a Muslim city. **T / F**

2. Only a few people of Ta'if became Muslims. **T / F**

3. Rasulullah (s.a.w.) went to the neighboring countries to preach Islam. **T / F**

4. Rasulullah (s.a.w.) sent teachers to the neighboring countries. **T / F**

5. Rasulullah (s.a.w.) preached Islam for fifty years. **T / F**

B. Fill in the blanks with the words given.

When Rasulullah (s.a.w.) began preaching Islam, there were few --------------- in the beginning. After ------------ years, almost all of the people of Arabia became Muslims. The Message of Islam also reached the neighboring ------.

(countries, Muslims, twenty-three)

Pilgrims praying at Jabal-ur-Rahmah

CHAPTER 15

THE FAREWELL SPEECH

Rasulullah (s.a.w.) knew that he would soon leave the world. He told his Ashab: "I want to go to Makkah to perform Hajj (Pilgrimage)." A large number of Muslims went with him. All of them loved him very much.

At Hajj, there were hundreds of thousands of people. All of them had come to worship Allah. Rasulullah (s.a.w.) thanked Allah for His blessings. Then, he asked the people: "O, people! have I given you Allah's Message?"

The people answered:
 O, Rasulullah! You have taught us the way of Islam, you have taught us the Qur'an. Truly, you have given us Allah's Message.

Rasulullah (s.a.w.) said:
 O, people! listen to me carefully. I may not be here to talk to you again. I have given you what Allah gave me. You must not forget Allah's message.

You must do good deeds. You must not do bad deeds. You should tell everyone about Islam. You should spread Allah's message.

No prophet will come after me. No new faith will be born.

I leave behind me two things, Al-Qur'an and Sunnah, my example. If you follow them, you will not fail.

After Hajj, Rasulullah (s.a.w.) spent most of his time in prayers. His health was not good. He became ill. Then his illness increased so much that he could not go to the Masjid.

He asked Abu Bakr to lead the Salat. His condition got worse every day. Finally, he passed away, to meet the Creator. At that time, he was saying, "Allah is the best Friend."

All of the Muslims were very sad. They did not want Rasulullah (s.a.w.) to leave them, but they knew it was the Will of Allah. "We will tell everyone about Rasulullah's teachings." they said.

****

Pilgrims at Jaddah Airport

Word Watch

farewell   Pilgrimage   thousands   condition
Sunnah

Thinking It Over

A. Circle the correct answer.

1. Rasulullah (s.a.w.) went to Makkah to perform Hajj ---------------
    a. with a few people.
    b. with a large number of people.
    c. all alone.

2. Rasulullah (s.a.w.) told the people ---------------
    a. "I have taught you my own ideas."
    b. "I have taught you the religion of your fathers."
    c. "I have taught you Allah's message."

3. During his illness, Rasulullah (s.a.w.) ordered --------------- to lead the Salat.
    a. Abu Bakr.
    b. Bilal ibn Ribah.
    c. Salman al-Farsi.

SAYINGS OF RASULULLAH

Islam is founded on five pillars:

1. Shahadah, bearing witness that there is no diety except Allah, and that Muhammad is His man and messenger.
2. Regular performance of Salat (prayers).
3. Zakat, the payment of poor-due.
4. Hajj (Pilgrimage).
5. Sawm, fasting in the month of Ramadan.

He, who greets first, is the closest to Allah.

When you enter a house, greet the people living in it, and when you leave a house, say your greetings.

The best in Islam is your feeding the poor and offering your greeting to the people you know and the people you do not know.

Cleanliness is a part of faith.

Seeking of knowledge is a duty of every male and female Muslim.

Whoever goes out to obtain knowledge is in Allah's path till he returns.

Make things easy and do not make them hard, and cheer people up.

Whoever wants to become the strongest of men, let him put his trust in Allah.

When anyone of you eats but forgets to remember Allah over his food, let him say: 'In the name of Allah, from the beginning to the end.'

When anyone of you eats, let him eat with his right hand and when he drinks, let him drink with his right hand.

Allah does not look at your bodies and your wealth, he looks at your hearts and deeds.

Whoever believes in Allah and the Day of Judgment, should honor his guest.

Allah may forgive all sins as He pleases except disobedience to parents.

The closest to Allah is the person who is kind to his family.

You shall not enter Paradise until you have faith, and you cannot have faith until you love one another.

He who does not love our youngers and does not respect our elders is not one of us.

Allah has no mercy on a person who is not kind to people.

He is not a believer who eats his full food while his neighbor is hungry.

It is not lawful for anyone to cut off relations with his brother for more than three days.

No Companion of mine should tell me anything bad about another.

A back-biter shall not enter Paradise.